BIPIN RAWAT

BIOGRAPHY OF AN ARMY MAN

TEAM INDUS

ISBN 979-888530516-7

This book is dedicated to Genral Bipin Rawat, Former Chief of Defence staff of India. We are deeply saddened by his untimely demise on 8 December 2021. He will always remain a true soldier of the Nation.

Contents

Preface   *vii*

    1. Early Life   1

    2. Military Career   3

    3. Personal Life   8

    4. Honours   9

    5. Demise   10

Tribute To A Hero   15

Preface

General Bipin Rawat (16 March 1958 – 8 December 2021) was an Indian military official who was a four-star general of the Indian Army. He filled in as the main Chief of Defense Staff (CDS) of the Indian Armed Forces from January 2020 until his demise in a helicopter crash in December 2021. Before taking over as the CDS, he filled in as the 57th and last Chairman of the Chiefs of Staff Committee just as 26th Chief of Army Staff of the Indian Army.

CHAPTER ONE

Early Life

Bipin Rawat was brought into the world in Pauri town of Pauri Garhwal region, current Uttarakhand state, on 16 March 1958. His family had been serving in the Indian Army for a considerable length of time. His dad Lakshman Singh Rawat (1930–2015) was from Sainj town of the Pauri Garhwal locale; dispatched into 11 Gorkha Rifles in 1951, he resigned as Deputy Chief of the Army Staff in 1988 as a lieutenant-general. His mom was from the Uttarkashi locale and was the little girl of Kishan Singh Parmar, the ex-Member of the Legislative Assembly (MLA) from Uttarkashi.

Rawat went to Cambrian Hall School in Dehradun and St. Edward's School in Shimla. He then, at that point, enlisted in the National Defense Academy, Khadakwasla and the Indian Military Academy, Dehradun, from where he graduated first in the request for merit and was granted the 'Blade of Honor'.

Rawat was additionally an alum of the Defense Services Staff College (DSSC), Wellington and the Higher Command Course at the United States Army Command and General Staff College (USACGSC) at Fort Leavenworth, Kansas in 1997. From his residency at the DSSC, he got a MPhil degree in Defense Studies just as confirmations in Management and Computer Studies from the University of Madras. In 2011, he was granted a privileged doctorate by CCS University, Meerut for his exploration on military-media vital examinations.

CHAPTER TWO

Military Career

Rawat was charged into the fifth legion, the 11 Gorkha Rifles (5/11 GR) on 16 December 1978, similar unit as his dad. During the 1987 Sino-Indian encounter in the Sumdorong Chu valley, then, at that point, Captain Rawat's regiment was sent against the Chinese People's Liberation Army. The deadlock was the principal military showdown along the contested McMahon Line after the 1962 conflict.

He has a lot of involvement with high-elevation fighting and went through ten years leading counter-insurrection activities. He told an organization in Uri, Jammu and Kashmir as a significant. As a colonel, he told his legion, the fifth contingent, the 11 Gorkha Rifles, in the eastern area along the Line of Actual Control at Kibithu. Elevated to the position of brigadier, he told 5 Sector of Rashtriya Rifles in Sopore.

Rawat directed MONUSCO (a Multinational Brigade in a Chapter VII mission in the Democratic Republic of the Congo). Inside about fourteen days of organization in the DRC, the Brigade confronted a significant hostile in the east which undermined the provincial capital of North Kivu, Goma. The hostile likewise took steps to undermine the nation in general. The circumstance requested a fast reaction and North Kivu Brigade was supported, where it was liable for more than 7,000 people, addressing almost 50% of the absolute MONUSCO power. While at the same time occupied with hostile dynamic tasks against the CNDP and other furnished gatherings, Rawat (then, at that point, Brigadier) completed strategic help to the Congolese Army (FARDC), He sharpening programs with the nearby populace and definite coordination to guarantee that all were educated with regards to the circumstance and cooperated in the advancement of activities. He was liable for the security of the weak populace. This functional period went on for a considerable length of time. Goma never fell, the East settled and the vitally equipped gathering was propelled to the arranging table and has since been coordinated into the FARDC. He was likewise entrusted to introduce the Revised Charter of Peace Enforcement to the Special Representatives of the Secretary-General and Force Commanders of all the UN missions in an uncommon gathering at Wilton Park, London, on 16 May 2009. Rawat was twice granted the Force Commander's Commendation.

After advancement to significant general, Rawat took over as the General Officer Commanding nineteenth Infantry Division (Uri). As a lieutenant general, he directed III Corps, settled in Dimapur, prior to assuming control over the Southern Army in Pune. He additionally held staff tasks which incorporated an educational residency at the Indian Military Academy (Dehradun), General Staff Officer Grade 2 at the Military Operations Directorate, coordinations staff official of a Re-coordinated Army Plains Infantry Division (RAPID) in focal India, Colonel Military Secretary and Deputy Military Secretary in the Military Secretary's Branch and Senior Instructor in the Junior Command Wing. He additionally filled in as the Major

General Staff (MGGS) of the Eastern Command.

In June 2015, eighteen Indian warriors were killed in a trap by aggressors having a place with the United Liberation Front of Western South East Asia (UNLFW) in Manipur. The Indian Army reacted with cross-line strikes in which units of the 21st legion of the Parachute Regiment struck a NSCN-K base in Myanmar. 21 Para was under the functional control of the Dimapur based III Corps, which was then instructed by Rawat. In the wake of being elevated to the Army Commander grade, Rawat expected the post of General Officer Commanding-in-Chief (GOC-in-C) Southern Command on 1 January 2016. After a short stretch, he expected the post of Vice Chief of Army Staff on 1 September 2016.

On 17 December 2016, the Government of India delegated Rawat as the 27th Chief of the Army Staff, overriding two more senior Lieutenant Generals, Praveen Bakshi and P. M. Hariz. The arrangement made by NDA administered Government was politically dubious. He got down to business of Chief of Army Staff as the 27th COAS on 31 December 2016, after retirement of General Dalbir Singh Suhag. He was the third official from the Gorkha Brigade to turn into the Chief of the Army Staff, after Field Marshal Sam Manekshaw and General Dalbir Singh Suhag.

In 2018, Rawat safeguarded the military Major associated with the Kashmir human safeguard occurrence, where a Kashmiri man was attached to a jeep as a human safeguard. The official was granted a Chief of Army Staff Commendation Card by Rawat for counter-revolt tasks. Rawat hosted been reprimanded by the resistance gathering pioneers for offering political expressions during the Citizenship Amendment Act fights.

On his visit to the United States in 2019, General Rawat was drafted to the United States Army Command and General Staff College International Hall of Fame. He was a privileged General of Nepalese Army as per the practice between the Indian and Nepali armed forces to present the privileged position of General upon one another's bosses to imply their nearby and extraordinary military ties.

Rawat filled in as the 57th and last Chairman of the Chiefs of Staff Committee. He filled in as the main Chief of Defense Staff (CDS) of the Indian Armed Forces from January 2020 until his passing in December 2021. India starting at 2021 had administration explicit orders framework. joint and coordinated orders, otherwise called bound together orders; and further separated into theater or useful orders, have been set up and more are proposed. In February 2020, Rawat said two to five auditorium orders might be set up. The fruition of the making of theater orders, both incorporated and joint orders, will require various years. Indian Air Force went against the arrangement of brought together auditorium orders refering to restriction of assets. In mid 2021, Rawat called the Indian Air Force a "supporting arm" of India's guard organization and framework. Air Chief Marshal R.K.S. Bhadauria offered a public expression accordingly that the IAF served a greater job than a supporting arm.

On 15 September 2021 while talking at an occasion in the limit of the CDS at the India International Center in New Delhi, General Rawat addressed the hypothesis of conflict of civilisations concerning the western civilisation and China's developing relations with nations like Iran and Turkey. The following day, on 16 September 2021, India's Minister of External Affairs S. Jaishankar passed on to his Chinese partner that India doesn't prefer any conflict of civilisations hypothesis.

CHAPTER THREE

Personal Life

In 1985, Rawat wedded Madhulika Raje Singh. A relative of a recent royal family, she was the little girl of Kunwar Mrigendra Singh, at some point Riyasatdar of the pargana of Sohagpur Riyasat in Shahdol area and an Indian National Congress MLA from the region in 1967 and 1972. She was instructed at Scindia Kanya Vidyalaya in Gwalior and graduated in brain research at Delhi University. The couple had two girls, Kritika and Tarini. Madhulika Rawat was the leader of the Army Wives Welfare Association (AWWA) during Bipin Rawat's residency as Chief of Army Staff. She turned into the leader of the Defense Wives Welfare Association (DWWA), upon the production of the post and the arrangement of General Bipin Rawat as the primary CDS. She attempted to make the spouses of protection faculty monetarily free. She was likewise engaged with NGOs and government assistance affiliations, for example, Veer Naris that helps widows of military work force, in an unexpected way abled kids and disease patients.

CHAPTER FOUR

Honours

During his career that has gone through more than 40 years, CdS General Bipin Rawat has received many medals and honors for distinguished service.

1- Param Vishisht Seva Medal

2- Uttam Yudh Seva Medal

3- Ati Vishisht Seva Medal

4- Yudh Seva Medal

5- Sena Medal

6- Vishisht Seva Medal

7- Wound Medal

8- Samanya Seva Medal

9- Special Service Medal

10- Operation Parakram Medal

11- Sainya Seva Medal

12- High Altitude Service Medal

13- Videsh Seva Medal

14- 50th Anniversary of Independence Medal

15- 30 Years Long Service Medal

16- 20 Years Long Service Medal

17- 9 Years Long Service Medal

18- MONUSCO

CHAPTER FIVE

Demise

On 8 December 2021, Rawat, his better half and individuals from his staff were among 10 travelers and 4 group individuals on board an Indian Air Force Mil Mi-17 helicopter flight on the way from the Sulur Airforce base to the Defense Services Staff College (DSSC), Wellington, where Rawat was to convey a talk. At around 12:10 p.m. neighborhood time, the airplane smashed close to a private settlement of private tea home workers on the edges of the village of Nanjappachatiram, Bandishola panchayat, in the Katteri-Nanchappanchathram space of Coonoor taluk, Nilgiris locale. The accident site was 10 km from the flight's expected objective. Rawat's passing – and those of his better half and 11 others – was subsequently affirmed by the Indian Air Force. Rawat's contact official, Group Captain Varun Singh was the last one standing. Rawat was 63 at the hour of his passing.

Rawat and his significant other were incinerated by Hindu customs with full military distinctions at Brar Square, New Delhi on 10 December 2021. They were agreed a 17 weapon salute. Their incineration was completed by their little girls, who took their remains to Haridwar and drenched them in the Ganges at the Har Ki Pauri ghat on 12 December.

On 8 December 2021, a Mil Mi-17V-5 vehicle helicopter worked by the Indian Air Force (IAF) slammed among Coimbatore and Wellington in Tamil Nadu, subsequent to withdrawing from Sulur Air Force Station. The helicopter was conveying Chief of Defense Staff General Bipin Rawat and 13 others, including his better half and staff. All individuals on board aside from one, a flying corps official, passed on in the accident. The Russian-assembled Mil Mi-17 medium-lift helicopter was one of the principal cluster of 80 of its sort worked for the IAF under the particulars of a 2008 agreement. Conveyed to the IAF in 2011 and drafted into administration in 2012, the helicopter had flown more than 26 hours without episode since its latest adjusting. Wing Commander Prithvi Singh Chauhan, the chief of 109 Helicopter Unit, was the pilot in order, with co-pilot Squadron Leader Kuldeep Singh and two junior warrant officials including the remainder of the group.

The travelers had loaded onto the trip around 11:45 a.m. nearby time. At 11:48 a.m. nearby time, the helicopter took off with 10 travelers and 4 team individuals from Sulur Air Force Station, headed about 80 km (50 mi) to the Defense Services Staff College (DSSC) in Wellington, Tamil Nadu. General Rawat, his better half and his staff were heading out to the DSSC, where Rawat was to address the school's personnel and understudy officials. The flight was booked to show up at Wellington by 12:15 p.m. Instantly prior to losing contact with the Sulur Air power base at 12:08 p.m., the pilots had radioed aviation authority to affirm their inescapable arriving at the Wellington helipad. The airplane then, at that point, smashed almost a private state of private tea bequest workers on the edges of the village of Nanjappachatiram, Bandishola panchayat, in the Katteri-

Nanchappanchathram space of Coonoor taluk, Nilgiris locale. The accident site was 10 km (6.2 mi) from the flight's expected objective.

As per an observer, he saw "the helicopter descending ... it hit one tree and was ablaze. There were crest of smoke" when he ran over. "In minutes, the fire was higher" than his home. Townspeople tossed water over the fire in endeavor to put it out. Starting reports of the accident arose around 12:20 p.m., with a hunt and-salvage activity dispatched at 12:25 p.m. The IAF formally affirmed General Rawat's quality on the trip in a tweet sent at 1:53 p.m. Salvage tasks proceeded until 3:25 p.m. Fire and Rescue Services work force who figured out how to arrive at the accident site after some trouble, as the site was 500 meters from a significant street, announced the accident casualties had been scorched to the point of being indistinguishable.

The ten travelers on board the flight included Chief of Defense Staff General Bipin Rawat, his better half Madhulika Rawat, contact official Group Captain Varun Singh and the overall's very own staff, involving his protection partner Brigadier Lakhbinder Singh Lidder, Lieutenant-Colonel Harjinder Singh and five NCOs. Following the accident, the IAF delivered articulations at 18:03 affirming the passing of 13 of the 14 individuals ready, including General Rawat and his significant other. As of 21:30 nearby time, each of the 13 of the bodies had been recuperated from the accident site.

An individual from the DSSC was the last one standing of the accident, and was taken to the tactical medical clinic in Wellington, Tamil Nadu, for medical procedure. Having supported consumes more than 45% of his body and in basic yet stable condition, he was accordingly moved to the Command Hospital in Bengaluru for additional treatment.

The Cabinet Committee on Security (CCS) headed by Prime Minister Narendra Modi met on the evening of the catastrophe to settle on a further strategy. The Minister of Defense Rajnath Singh made a proper declaration in Parliament on 9 December in regards to the episode. The Opposition suspended its fights in Parliament for one day as an accolade for the people who lost their lives in the accident. The flight information recorder was recuperated on the morning of 9 December. A tri-administration commission of request was set up by the IAF, headed via Air Marshal Manavendra Singh, the AOC-in-C Training Command.

Tribute To A Hero

General Bipin Rawat, 1st Chief of Defence Staff

9 7 9 8 8 8 5 3 0 5 1 6 7